The In-Sync Activity Card Book

A book version of *The In-Sync Activity Cards*

Joye Newman, MA, and Carol Kranowitz, MA

Based on their book

Growing an In-Sync Child: Simple, Fun Activities to Help Every Child Develop, Learn, and Grow

The In-Sync Activity Card Book

All marketing and publishing rights guaranteed to and reserved by:

800•489•0727

Online: www.sensoryworld.com

Email: info@sensoryworld.com

Table of Contents

Intermediate Activities

Advanced Activities

About *The In-Sync Activity Card Book*

Each activity is:

Developmentally based. The activities are organized into three levels:

- Beginner—skills of a typically developing preschooler

- Intermediate—skills of a typically developing primary-school child

- Advanced—skills of a typically developing elementary-school child

In addition, all activities include suggestions for more challenging moves as kids develop more skills.

Flexible and adaptable. Each activity includes ways to customize the movement experiences to suit your child's specific needs. Because your child is unique, is better at some moves than others, has definite preferences, and does not want to do the same old exercises day after day, please feel free to get creative!

Addressing many skills simultaneously. Rather than concentrating on one skill at a time, these activities incorporate many basic sensory, motor, and visual skills. The primary skills addressed are listed on each activity.

Let's get started!

- Determine where your child's skill level lies on the continuum, from beginner to advanced. Remember, these levels are flexible and are merely guidelines.

- Just dig in! If the activity you choose is too easy, we offer ways to make it more challenging. If it is too hard, choose another one.

Our hope is that you will quickly customize the program to suit you and your child's needs by integrating your own personal touches.

Remember—it takes only a few minutes each day to give your child moving experiences that will last a lifetime.

Movement Gets Us in Sync!

Pediatricians, teachers, and other specialists now recognize that early motor development is vital to a child's physical, emotional, academic, and overall success. When children play outside, climb trees, jump in puddles, and roll down hills, they develop these essential sensory, perceptual, and visual skills.

Sensory Skills

Tactile processing is receiving sensations through the skin and hair and responding to those sensations. A child whose brain accurately interprets tactile input is comfortable being touched by other people or objects.

Vestibular processing is taking in sensations about gravity through the inner ear and responding to these sensations. The child learns where her head is relative to the surface of the earth—whether she is upright, lying down, or falling.

Proprioception is the unconscious awareness of sensations coming from muscles and joints. The child learns whether he is stomping or tiptoeing, how hard to press a pencil, and how to stretch out his arm to open a door.

Perceptual Skills

Balance, both static (being in place) and dynamic (moving), helps a child remain seated or hop across the room.

Bilateral coordination is the ability to move both sides of the body simultaneously, to jump on both feet or steady a paper while writing.

Directionality is awareness of up, down, forward, backward, sideways, and diagonal movement and the ability to move in these directions on command.

Laterality is awareness of two sides of the body and the ability to move either side independently of the other.

Midline crossing is the ability to use a hand, foot, or eye across the center of the body. Crossing the midline is especially important for integrating two sides of the body, as well as two sides of the world.

Motor planning is the ability to organize and sequence the steps of an unfamiliar and complex body movement in a coordinated manner.

Spatial awareness is the understanding of space and "where one is" relative to the surrounding world. Children become aware of spatial relationships by moving through space. A child who crawls across the room learns more about spatial dimensions than one who is carried.

Visual Skills

Vision, binocularity, and visual tracking are important developmental skills. A task such as writing, climbing stairs, and catching a ball requires your child to integrate many complicated skills and abilities.

———

Your child can acquire these fundamental skills only by moving. Use this book to give your child a head start and a leg up! Have fun!

For more detailed discussion, see *Growing an In-Sync Child: Simple, Fun Activities to Help Every Child Develop, Learn, and Grow*, by Kranowitz and Newman.

Get In Sync—in Seconds!

Use this chart as a reference for designing your own instant In-Sync activity. Begin by choosing one word from each of the first four columns, such as, "Walk forward, way up high, in a straight line." Change just one word in any of these columns to make a different activity, like, "Jump forward, way up high, in a straight line." Now, have fun by changing one or more words and by integrating words from as many columns as you want. Feel free to add your own words to make every activity different and fun!

MOVEMENT	DIRECTION	LEVEL	PATHWAY	TEMPO	DYNAMIC	ENHANCEMENT
Walk	Forward	High	Straight	Fast	Loud	Balance beanbag
Run	Backward	Medium	Curved	Slow	Soft	Roll ball
Jump	Toward target	Low	Zigzag	Medium		Bounce ball
Hop	Diagonally		Spiral			
Roll						
Leap						
Gallop						
Slide						
Creep						
Wiggle						

Helpful Hints

In-Sync activities will be most successful when you follow these helpful hints:

1. Your voice can be a very powerful tool. Inflection and intonation can change the entire aspect of the activity. Use your voice playfully, softly, or excitedly to add a new dimension to your directions.

2. When appropriate, ask your child to fix his gaze on a visual target in front of him, such as a lamp, a line of masking tape, or even you! Adding a visual target can enhance your child's balance, posture, and attention.

3. Be aware of your child's breathing. Frequently, people hold their breath when concentrating. Have your child count with you or continue a conversation to keep her breathing even.

4. When referring to limbs as "right" or "left," remember to demonstrate by using your opposite hand or foot. As your child faces you, his right hand will mirror your left hand.

Body Baton

What You Need

Miniature or larger trampoline

Hands for clapping or rhythm sticks, drum, or tambourine

What You Do

1. Say, "Step up on the trampoline. I'll be the conductor, and your jumping body will be orchestra. When I clap my hands (beat my drum) slowly, you will jump slowly. When I clap fast, you'll jump fast. Let's go."

2. Say, "Now, you will be the conductor. Your jumping body will be the baton. It will tell me how fast or slowly to clap my hands. Start conducting!"

Helps Your Child Develop and Enhance …

- Auditory processing (for recognizing verbal social cues)

- Proprioception (for knowing when to press hard or lightly on a crayon or pencil)

- Vestibular processing (for sitting at a desk)

Ways to Make It More Challenging

- Change your clapping tempo rapidly.

- Gradually change from slow to fast to slow.

- Together, compile a list of songs, rhymes, and chants to accompany the jumping.

What to Look for

- Your child discriminates the differences in your changing tempos.

- He changes his own jumping and clapping tempos and recognizes gradations between fast and slow.

Beginner

Car Wash

What You Need

A length of rope that stretches across the room

Crepe paper streamers or lengths of ribbon or yarn

What You Do

1. Cut pieces of crepe paper or ribbon approximately 8 feet long. Tie these pieces around the rope so they will hang down when the rope is stretched horizontally across the room.

2. Tie one end of the rope to a doorknob. Hold the other end.

3. Say, "Show me how you can go through this car wash." Watch your child move back and forth, under the rope and through the streamers.

4. Ask him to move through the car wash in various ways:

   - On his tummy

   - On his back

   - Jumping on two feet

Helps Your Child Develop and Enhance …

- Motor planning (for drying off with a towel)

- Tactile processing (for washing with a loofah or a washcloth)

Ways to Make It More Challenging

- Hold the rope at different angles. Challenge your child to go under the high side or the low side of the car wash.

- Gently shake the rope as he goes through the car wash.

What to Look for

- He enjoys the feel of the streamers as he goes through the car wash.

- He moves as requested.

Clap Your Feet

What You Need

A place to sit

What You Do

1. Say, "Can you clap your hands? Yes, you can! Great! Now, can you clap your feet?"

2. Continue:

   - Shake head, shake hand

   - Nod head, nod pointer finger

   - Roll hands, roll feet

   - Wiggle thumb, wiggle big toe

   - Scrunch face, scrunch hands and feet

   - Open and close mouth, and then two fingers

Helps Your Child Develop and Enhance …

- Auditory processing (for responding quickly to directions)

- Body awareness (for putting shoes on the correct feet)

- Motor planning (for getting into the car seat)

Ways to Make It More Challenging

- Ask your child to copy your movements without any verbal directions.

- Have her suggest other movements to do with other body parts.

- Ask her to "pair" movements, such as clapping her hands and feet at the same time.

What to Look for

- She responds quickly and accurately to your instructions.

- She makes simultaneous movements when called for.

Beginner

Copy Cat

What You Need

No equipment

What You Do

1. Stand facing your child and say, "Watch what I do and then copy me."

2. Raise your hand straight over your head and bring it out to your side and down to your thigh in a great semicircle. Say, "Now, you do it."

3. Say, "Here comes another move. Watch." Balance on one foot and wiggle your other foot.

4. Continue moving your arms, legs, and head in various ways for him to imitate.

5. Now let him lead, and you be the copy cat.

Helps Your Child Develop and Enhance …

- Body awareness (for placing his feet on the bike pedals)

- Motor planning (for using his feet to pedal and his hands to steer the bike)

- Visual processing (for anticipating when to turn, how to avoid obstacles, and how to stop and go on the bike path)

Ways to Make It More Challenging

- Have your child mirror your movements simultaneously, rather than waiting to start until you've finished a move.

- Play "Copy Can't," by having him do the opposite of your move. For example, if you reach way up high with one hand, he will reach down low with his hand.

What to Look for

- Your child's movements match yours accurately.

- He initiates novel movements when he is the leader.

Floppy Noodle

What You Need

No equipment

What You Do

1. Say, "Show me how you reach all the way up to the sky." Demonstrate as you stretch your arms as high as possible.

2. Say, "Now, put your hands on your toes, like this. Let's 'walk' our hands up to our knees, up our thighs, over our tummies, up our chests to our chins, across our mouths, noses, and eyes, up our foreheads and all the way up to the sky."

3. Say, "Let's stretch WAY up to the sky, stretch, stretch. Now, be a floppy noodle! Bend at your waist, letting your upper body flop and bounce."

4. Say, "Put your hands on your toes. Now let's 'jump' our hands up to our knees, up our thighs, over our tummies, up our chests to our chins, across our mouths, noses, and eyes, up our foreheads and all the way up to the sky."

5. Repeat step #3, stretching up and then becoming a floppy noodle.

6. Repeat steps #2 and #3, using these movement words:

   - Tiptoe

   - March

   - Slide

Helps Your Child Develop and Enhance …

- Bilateral coordination (for breaking up dry spaghetti to drop into the pot)

- Proprioception (for getting the cooked spaghetti onto her fork)

- Vestibular processing (for tilting her head back to suck in long strands of spaghetti)

Ways to Make It More Challenging

- Use only one hand at a time.

- Ask your child to be a "floppy noodle" all on her own.

What to Look for

- She moves her hands appropriately.

- She stretches way up high.

- She flops easily, relaxing her upper body and head.

Hold Up the Wall

What You Need

A wall

What You Do

1. Say, "Oh, let's pretend the wall is falling! Quick! Let's hold up the wall!"

2. Press your hands against the wall. Say, "You press your hands against the wall, too! Push, harder!"

3. Ask, "What else shall we press against the wall? Our backs? Right!"

4. Continue pushing the wall with other body parts.

Helps Your Child Develop and Enhance …

- Bilateral coordination (for pulling up her pants)

- Body awareness (for putting the right arm in the right sleeve)

- Proprioception (for pulling on her boots)

Ways to Make It More Challenging

- Have your child press one body part at a time against the wall, such as one hand, one shoulder, one foot, and one knee (and so on).

- Have her press two different body parts against the wall simultaneously, such as one hand and one knee.

- Have her do this activity while you tell her—but not show her!—what to do.

- Have her be the leader.

What to Look for

- She quickly locates the correct body part(s).

- She pushes the specified body parts against the wall.

Beginner

Hoopscotch

What You Need

Six to nine Hula-hoops

Chalk or masking tape

Chalkboard or large piece of paper

Beanbag

What You Do

1. Ask your child to set up the hoops on the driveway (or floor) in a 1, 2, 1, 2 pattern.

2. If outdoors, use chalk to write the numbers 1 through 9 in the hoops, beginning with the first hoop on the left as "1" (see illustration). If indoors, use masking tape to form the numbers in the hoops.

3. Say, "Can you jump with your feet apart into the hoops when they're next to each other, and with your feet together into the single hoops? Then hop back." Demonstrate if necessary.

4. Ask your child to toss the beanbag into one of the hoops.

5. Ask her to jump to the hoop in which she tossed the beanbag, pick up the beanbag, and jump back.

6. Ask her to write the number of the hoop from which she retrieved the beanbag on the chalkboard, paper, or driveway.

7. Continue until all the numbers from 1 through 9 have been written down or until your child decides she's done.

Helps Your Child Develop and Enhance …

- Balance (for riding a bike)

- Bilateral coordination (for pumping her legs and holding on when swinging)

- Laterality (for galloping)

- Spatial awareness (for running to first base in baseball)

Ways to Make It More Challenging

- Have her write the numbers 1 through 9 on the chalkboard or paper before she begins the game. Then she can erase or cross out the numbers as she retrieves the beanbag.

- Have her hop on one foot into the single hoops.

What to Look for

- She jumps in and out of the hoops neatly.

- She is mostly accurate when throwing the beanbag into the hoops.

- Both her feet touch the ground simultaneously when she jumps.

Beginner

Hoopy Day

What You Need

A Hula-hoop big enough to stand in

What You Do

1. Ask your child to place the hoop on the floor and stand in it.

2. Say, "Show me how to …"

   - Put your nose outside the hoop.

   - Put two feet out of the hoop and keep the rest of you in the hoop.

   - Put just one elbow and one knee outside the hoop.

   - Put only your head outside the hoop.

3. Ask your child to put one foot in the hoop and one foot out of the hoop and then:

   - Jump around the hoop

   - Reverse direction

   - Tiptoe around the hoop forward and backward

4. Ask him to put one hand in the hoop and one foot outside the hoop. Repeat the directions as in #3.

5. Continue asking him to place various body parts in and out of the hoop, moving in different and fun ways.

Helps Your Child Develop and Enhance …

- Body awareness (for dressing himself)

- Motor planning (for coordinating one movement with another)

- Spatial awareness (for playing hide-and-seek)

Ways to Make It More Challenging

Ask your child to:

- Keep his chin in the hoop and the rest of himself out of the hoop.

- Place one hand and one foot on the floor outside the hoop, and move forward and backward around the hoop.

- Show you his own way to move around the hoop, using words to describe how he will be moving.

What to Look for

- He locates and moves his body parts as requested.

- He can isolate his specific body parts accurately, as requested.

Jumpland

What You Need

Masking tape, chalk, or twigs

A low step or sandbox rim

What You Do

1. Have your child stand on a low step. Ask, "How far can you jump? Land on both feet, and I'll mark the spot with masking tape (or chalk/twig)."

2. Say, "Look how far you jumped! That's great! Now, look at the mark and jump even farther."

3. Continue encouraging her to extend her jumps, marking each landing.

Helps Your Child Develop and Enhance …

- Bilateral coordination (for catching a beach ball)

- Proprioception (for jumping over waves at the beach)

- Spatial awareness (for building sand castles)

Ways to Make It More Challenging

- Before your child jumps, have her put a marker on the ground as her goal.

- Have her jump from a flat starting point.

What to Look for

- She has sufficient "oomph" to propel herself forward.

- She recognizes the visual markers.

Beginner

Levitation

What You Need

A chair

What You Do

1. Have your child sit in a chair and place her hands on the edges.

2. Say, "Push downward with your hands and lift your bottom off the seat. Great! Come down slowly. Do it again, a few more times."

3. Say, "You are so strong! You are defying gravity!"

Helps Your Child Develop and Enhance …

- Balance (for riding a scooter)

- Bilateral coordination (for jumping rope)

- Proprioception (for climbing a tree)

Ways to Make It More Challenging

- Have her "levitate" in different chairs.

- Have her levitate her body and hold it in midair for a count of three.

- Have her do 10 levitations.

What to Look for

- Your child has sufficient upper-body strength to raise her body from the chair.

- She pushes herself straight up, rather than forward.

- She lowers her body slowly to the seat.

Look and Be

What You Need

Chalk and chalkboard

What You Do

1. Say, "I'm going to draw a star on the chalkboard. When I point to it, show me how you can make your body look like a star."

2. Say, "I'm going to draw some more things on the board. Show me how you can make your whole body look like each of these drawings." Then draw objects such as:

   - Table
   - Bowl
   - Egg
   - Tree

3. Say, "When I point to one of these drawings, you make your body into that shape." Point to one shape at a time in random order, as your child practices being an egg and then a tree. Go slowly.

Helps Your Child Develop and Enhance …

- Body awareness (for knowing which foot goes in which boot)

- Motor planning (for getting her arms into her jacket sleeves)

- Visual processing (for finding her mittens in the closet)

Ways to Make It More Challenging

- Have your child think of other categories and get into different positions on your command, such as:

  - Outdoors: mountain, river, highway, cloud

  - Sports: skier, car racer, bicyclist, baseball pitcher

  - Critters: worm, spider, bird, cat

- Change the game to "Hear and Be." Instead of pointing to an icon, say a word (e.g., "star") and ask her to take that shape. Make this even more challenging by having her move around the space in various ways as she listens for your command.

What to Look for

- She maneuvers her body into different positions that generally correspond to the suggested shape.

- She recognizes the position you want with her eyes and ears.

Beginner

Me and My Shadow

What You Need

Sidewalk and chalk or brown paper and crayon

Beanbag

What You Do

1. Ask your child to lie down on the sidewalk (or paper). Say, "Now, I'm going to trace around your whole body. We'll call this your shadow."

2. Once his outline is drawn, say, "OK, stand up. Put the beanbag on your shadow's head. Now, put it on your shadow's tummy."

3. Continue having him place the beanbag on his shadow's body parts as you call them out.

4. Say, "Now I'm going to touch you somewhere on your real body. Put the beanbag on the same place on your shadow."

Helps Your Child Develop and Enhance …

- Body awareness (for hiding behind a tree)

- Directionality (for running toward the goal)

- Tactile processing (for knowing where he's been tagged)

- Visual processing (for using a treasure map)

Ways to Make It More Challenging

- Touch your child on two body parts simultaneously and place two beanbags on his shadow.

- Have him trace your body and reverse roles.

What to Look for

- He accurately identifies body parts on himself from your verbal cues.

- He places the beanbag correctly on his shadow.

Beginner

Move on Up

What You Need

No equipment

What You Do

1. Stand facing your child and say, "Let's pretend we are climbing a ladder. Watch how high I can stretch my arm into the air. Can you do it, too?" Stretch your left arm as high as you can. Remember that when you're facing him, you will use your left arm when he uses his right arm.

2. Say, "Now, while our right arms are in the air, let's raise our left knees, like this." Raise your right knee; your child raises his left.

3. Say, "Let's count to five while we stay like this."

4. Repeat, switching sides.

Helps Your Child Develop and Enhance …

- Balance (for standing while fishing)

- Laterality (for reeling in the fish)

- Proprioception (for knowing when the fish has been hooked)

Ways to Make It More Challenging

- Have your child "climb" the ladder with his eyes closed.

- Have him spell words instead of counting as he maintains his position.

What to Look for

- He maintains his balance while in position.

- He raises the appropriate limbs.

Beginner

Over and Under

What You Need

Beanbag

What You Do

1. Say, "Show me how you can be next to the beanbag. Good! Now be in front of the beanbag."

2. Continue giving directions, using a different preposition each time:

- In back of
- Under
- Around
- Over
- In

Helps Your Child Develop and Enhance ...

- Auditory processing (for following the teacher's verbal directions)

- Directionality (for knowing where to put her name on her paper)

- Motor planning (for playing on the playground at recess)

- Spatial awareness (for finding the way to her desk in a crowded classroom)

Ways to Make It More Challenging

- Substitute furniture, park benches, puddles, and other objects for the beanbag.

- Include "right" and "left" in your directions:

  - "Put your right hand under the beanbag."

  - "Stand next to the table and put your left hand on top."

  - "Put your left elbow above the doorknob."

What to Look for

- Your child understands the prepositions and responds without hesitation.

- She gets her body into the correct position.

Paint the Town

What You Need

Wide painter's brush and pail

What You Do

1. Give the empty bucket to your child outdoors and say, "Let's get some water." Be sure he fills the bucket only part way, so he will be able to carry it.

2. Say, "Now, carry the bucket over here." Direct your child to an outside wall of the house or shed.

3. Give him the paintbrush and say, "Show me how you can paint the house."

4. Say, "Show me how you paint the house with up-and-down strokes. Great!"

5. Say, "Show me how you paint the house with side-to-side strokes. Terrific!"

Helps Your Child Develop and Enhance …

- Laterality (for playing the violin)

- Midline crossing (for playing the timpani)

- Proprioception (for striking the gong)

Ways to Make It More Challenging

- Let him fill the pail with more water, making it heavier.

- Give him two brushes of different widths. Ask him to paint with each hand individually and then with both together.

- Have him paint shapes and letters on a wall.

What to Look for

- Your child carries the bucket.

- He paints with big, broad strokes.

Beginner

Paper Clips

What You Need

Note cards and colored paper clips

What You Do

1. Place several paper clips on one edge of a note card. Say, "Can you arrange these clips on your card so they are in the same pattern as mine?"

2. Keep rearranging the paperclips, making the patterns more difficult by:

   - Using more clips

   - Placing the clips on two or more edges of the card

Helps Your Child Develop and Enhance ...

- Laterality (for writing)

- Tactile processing (for holding a pencil)

- Visual processing (for writing on the lines)

Ways to Make It More Challenging

- Begin a pattern with the paper clips. Ask your child to continue the pattern.

- Call out the colors for him to use, such as red, blue, yellow, green.

What to Look for

- He places the clips on the card.

- He recreates the patterns as requested.

Pass the Salt

What You Need

Three or more people around a table

A salt shaker

What You Do

1. Sit to the right of your child and say, "Can you reach the salt and pass it to me? Use the same hand to pass it to me that you used to reach for it. Thank you."

2. Take the salt from her with one hand and use that same hand to pass it to another person on your right, saying, "Here's the salt. Please take it with one hand and pass it to the next person with the same hand. We're going to pass the salt around the table, using just one hand."

3. Once the salt gets back to you, say, "Now we're going to do the same thing, but going in the other direction."

4. Pass the salt to your child, and continue around the table until it gets back to you.

Helps Your Child Develop and Enhance …

- Directionality (for turning faucets on and off)

- Laterality (for brushing her teeth)

- Midline crossing (for putting on an earring)

Ways to Make It More Challenging

- Pass the salt with four fingers—two from each hand.

- Pass a heavier object that would require the use of both hands.

What to Look for

- Your child uses the same hand to pass the salt as she used to receive it.

- She keeps it going in the correct direction.

Beginner

Repeat My Beat

What You Need

A surface to bang on (table, drum, floor, thighs)

What You Do

1. Sit beside your child at the table. Say, "Listen to the sounds my hands make on the table." Tap your hands, one, two, one, two, in a slow and steady rhythm.

2. Say, "Make your hands do what my hands are doing. Repeat my beat."

3. When your child is successful, beat your hands again, this time a little faster. Ask him to repeat your beat.

4. Say, "You got it! Now, it's your turn. Make a beat that I can repeat."

5. Continue taking turns and making the patterns increasingly complex, varying tempo and rhythm.

Helps Your Child Develop and Enhance …

- Auditory processing (for differentiating everyday sounds)

- Laterality (for pointing)

- Proprioception (for pulling a wagon)

Ways to Make It More Challenging

- Repeat each other's beat by using other body parts:

    - Feet stomping or jumping

    - Elbows striking your sides

    - Fingers tapping puffed cheeks

- Beat out familiar tunes and challenge each other to recognize them, such as "I've Been Working on the Railroad."

What to Look for

- Your child repeats your beat accurately.

- His tapping is strong and audible.

- His patterns are recognizable.

Scurry Scavenger Hunt

What You Need

Objects in your surrounding environment

What You Do

1. Say, "Look around. When I say, 'Go,' scurry around and touch five blue things with your finger, as fast as you can. Then come back to me. Ready? Go."

2. Once your child has touched five blue things, change the body part from finger to nose. Change the category from blue to round things. Say, "When I say, 'Go,' jump on two feet and put your nose on three round things. Ready? Go!"

3. Continue in this manner, changing the locomotor skills, the category, and the body part. For example:

   - "Hop around and use your elbow to touch things with straight lines."

   - "Roll around and use your knee to touch things that are square."

4. Let her give the directions.

Helps Your Child Develop and Enhance …

- Body awareness (for tagging someone "out" in softball)

- Spatial awareness (for pitching into the strike zone)

- Visual processing (for knowing when and where to throw the ball)

Ways to Make It More Challenging

- Use more complex directions, such as, "Jump to something blue, put your nose on it, then roll to something green, and put your toes on it."

- Ask her to map out with pencil and paper the path she took to locate her objects.

What to Look for

- She moves in the way requested.

- She finds the correct objects.

- She uses the right body part as named.

Beginner

Treasure Trove

What You Need

Plastic tub

Enough beans or sand to fill the tub ⅔ full

Treasures, such as coins, buttons, small cars, and paper clips

What You Do

1. Pour the beans or sand into the tub.

2. Show your child the collection of treasures and have him bury them deeply in the tub.

3. Say, "Put your hands into the tub and take out two coins."

4. Have him immerse his hands to find more treasures.

Helps Your Child Develop and Enhance …

- Tactile processing (for tying his shoes and keyboarding)

- Visual processing (for tying his shoes and keyboarding without looking)

Ways to Make It More Challenging

- Have your child tell you what he's found before taking it out of the tub.

- Give him more complex directions, such as, "Find a coin and a car."

What to Look for

- He successfully finds the treasures.

- He enjoys having his hands in the tub.

Cheery Cheerleader

What You Need

Pairs of pom-poms, t-shirts, or socks

What You Do

1. Give your child a pair of pom-poms and ask her to shake them:

   • Over her head

   • In front of her body

   • To her sides

   • Behind her back

2. Say, "Now let's pretend the pom-poms are a paint brush. Can you paint circles with them?" Give the same suggestions as in step #1.

3. Have her use her pom-poms to paint:

- Squares

- Triangles

- Horizontal and vertical lines

Helps Your Child Develop and Enhance …

- Bilateral coordination (for using a paint roller on the wall)

- Proprioception (for stirring the paint)

- Spatial awareness (for knowing where to paint)

Ways to Make It More Challenging

- Have her "paint" more complex shapes, such as figure eights and stars.

- Have her paint shapes with one hand at a time. Be sure she switches hands.

What to Look for

- She uses strong arms to shake her pom-poms.

- She understands the spatial concepts.

- She paints the shapes relatively accurately.

Intermediate

Come Here, Thumb

What You Need

No equipment

What You Do

1. While your child lies on her back, say, "Clasp your hands together and hold them way up toward the sky. Keep them clasped and hold up one thumb. Keep looking at your thumb as you slowly bring your hands toward your nose."

2. When her thumb gets about 4 inches from her nose, say, "Good! Now keep watching that thumb and slowly push your hands away."

3. Watch her eyes to make sure they move toward each other (inward) as her hands approach her nose. Her eyes should straighten as she pushes her hands away.

4. Repeat five times.

5. Once she successfully uses clasped hands, ask her to repeat steps #1 through #3 with just one hand at a time. Be sure to repeat this activity the same number of times with each hand. End this activity as it began, with your child using both hands together.

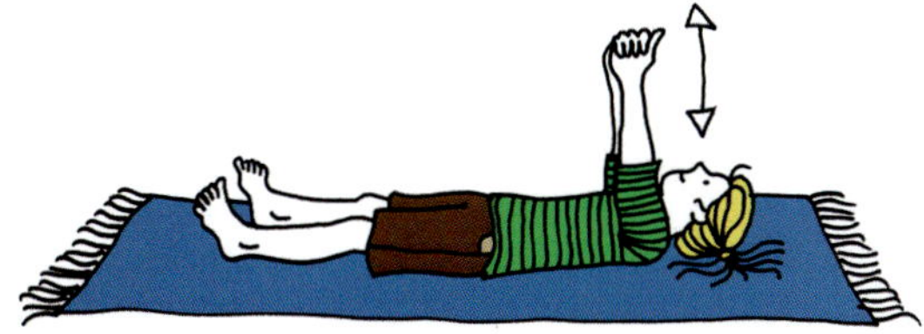

Helps Your Child Develop and Enhance ...

- Proprioception (for flexing and extending limbs slowly or quickly)

- Visual processing (for watching objects as they come closer and move farther away)

Ways to Make It More Challenging

- Have her inhale deeply as she brings her finger toward her nose and exhale as she pushes her finger away.

- Have her do this activity while seated in a chair with both feet on the ground.

- Have her do this activity while standing.

- Place three or four small colored beads on a 12-inch string and tie one end of the string to a door handle. (This is called a "Brock String.") Have her hold the other end of the string on the bridge of her nose. Ask her to look at the beads in order, from the farthest one near the door to the bead nearest her nose.

What to Look for

- Your child moves her hands slowly and smoothly toward and away from her nose.

- Her eyes move smoothly toward and away from each other.

Intermediate

Creepinator

What You Need

No equipment

What You Do

1. Say, "Show me how you can creep across the room on your hands and knees. How slowly can you go?"

2. Say, "Now, creep again, this time sliding your hands along the floor as you go. Your knees will still lift off the floor. Now you are a brand new creature called 'Creepinator!'"

3. Have your child be a Creepinator all around the house.

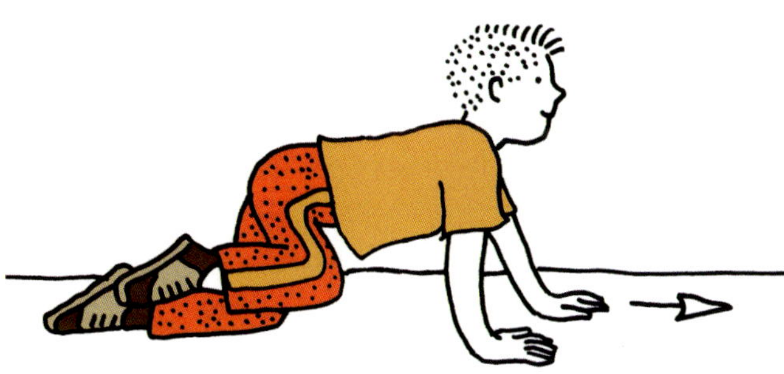

Helps Your Child Develop and Enhance …

- Laterality (for pulling a pillow out of the pillowcase)

- Motor planning (for changing the sheets)

- Tactile processing (for smoothing wrinkles out of a bedspread)

Ways to Make It More Challenging

- Ask your child to creep and slide his hands as he moves backward.

- Have him creep and slide on different surfaces, such as carpet, tile, and grass.

What to Look for

- He uses opposite hands and knees as he creeps.

- He slides his hands on the floor, although his knees continue to lift off the floor.

Intermediate

Fun 52 Pickup

What You Need

Deck of cards

What You Do

1. Hand your child a deck of cards and say, "Toss these cards up in the air so they fall all over the floor."

2. Say, "Turn over the cards so you can see all the numbers and faces."

3. Say, "Jump on two feet and bring me…"

   - Four aces

   - Eight red cards

   - Seven spades

4. Have him move in different ways to retrieve the cards:

   - Roll

   - Hop

   - Creep

   - Scootch

Helps Your Child Develop and Enhance …

- Auditory processing (for following directions)

- Vestibular processing (for bending over to pull weeds)

- Visual processing (for differentiating between weeds and flowers)

Ways to Make It More Challenging

- Give your child more complex instructions, such as, "Bring me two aces, four spades, and a black card."

- Have him practice his math skills by saying, "Bring me three cards that add up to 11."

What to Look for

- He picks up the appropriate cards.

- He responds appropriately to the movement instructions.

Intermediate

Jokers Are Wild

What You Need

Deck of cards

What You Do

1. Separate the face cards from the rest of the deck.

2. Show the face cards to your child. Together, decide that each card will represent a different movement, such as:

   - Jack = jump

   - Queen = clap hands behind back

   - King = squat

   - Joker = any movement of his choosing

3. Scatter the remaining cards on the floor, face down. Hold the face cards in your hand so your child can't see them.

4. Say, "Pick a card from my hand. Now choose a card from the floor. The face card will tell you the movement to do, and the number card will tell you how many times to do it." For example, if he chooses the six of spades and the queen of hearts, he will clap his hands behind his back six times.

5. Repeat a few more times.

Helps Your Child Develop and Enhance …

- Bilateral coordination (for bunting the baseball)

- Motor planning (for hitting and running)

- Visual processing (for interpreting the plays on the field)

Ways to Make It More Challenging

- Have him choose two number cards and add them together to determine the number of repetitions.

- Introduce more difficult movements.

What to Look for

- He translates the cards into movements.

- He is accurate in his counting.

Intermediate

Jump Up

What You Need

Tennis ball

What You Do

1. Say, "Show me how you can jump up and down in the same place."

2. Say, "Now I'm going to roll this ball toward you. Show me how you can jump straight up in the air so the ball rolls right under your feet. Make sure your feet land at the same time. Ready?"

3. Roll the ball slowly toward your child's feet.

4. Say, "Each time I roll the ball, jump up. When the ball rolls under your feet without being touched, you get a point. How many points shall we score?"

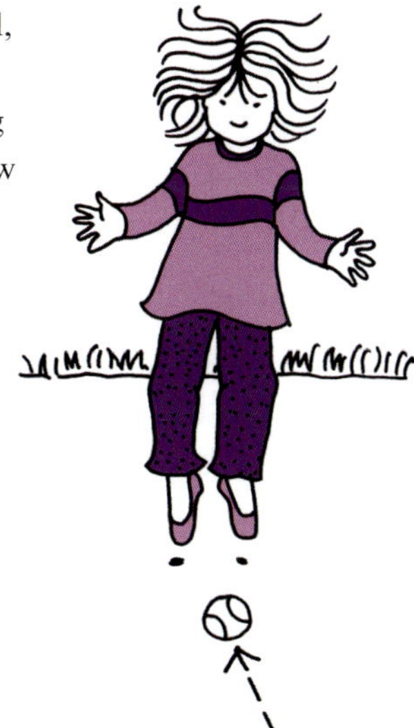

Helps Your Child Develop and Enhance ...

- Bilateral coordination (for doing push-ups and jumping jacks)

- Spatial awareness (for maneuvering through obstacles)

- Visual processing (for passing the ball to a teammate)

Ways to Make It More Challenging

- Roll the ball faster.

- Try to trick her by rolling the ball just enough to reach her, so it barely touches her feet. Say, "If you see that the ball is not going to roll under your feet, don't jump!"

- Use a bigger ball.

What to Look for

- She jumps on both feet simultaneously.

- She accurately judges the path of the ball.

Intermediate

KP Duty

What You Need

Peelable vegetables, such as carrots, cucumbers, and potatoes

Vegetable peeler

What You Do

1. Say, "I need your help in the kitchen. Let's peel these vegetables."

2. Show your child how to hold the carrot with one hand and scrape away from himself with the other hand. Let him experiment to see which hand peels better.

Helps Your Child Develop and Enhance …

- Laterality (for using scissors)

- Proprioception (for squeezing glue out of the container)

- Tactile processing (for doing messy art projects)

Ways to Make It More Challenging

- Have him sing a song as he peels.

- Have him scrape the peelings into a container.

What to Look for

- He uses the peeler properly.

- He enjoys himself.

Listen and Draw

What You Need

Newsprint

Crayons (not markers)

Recorded instrumental music without lyrics

What You Do

1. Play some instrumental (not vocal) music, such as classical pieces or jazz. Tape newsprint to the wall and put a container of crayons near it.

2. Ask your child to draw the way the music inspires him.

3. Remind him, if necessary, that he will get stronger colors when he presses firmly on the crayons.

4. Change the paper and the music. Choose music with varied tempos, rhythms, and moods.

Helps Your Child Develop and Enhance …

- Auditory processing (for tuning his guitar)

- Proprioception (for strumming)

- Tactile processing (for placing his fingers on the frets)

Ways to Make It More Challenging

- Have him use the other hand to draw.

- Have him balance on something like a telephone book or sturdy shoebox.

What to Look for

- Your child's crayon lines vary according to the type of music he is listening to.

- He varies the pressure on the crayons (to get strong or light colors) without breaking them.

Intermediate

More Core

What You Need

A wall

What You Do

1. Say, "Let's practice sitting taller. Let's sit against the wall. We'll stick our legs straight out, with our toes pointing to the sky, and press our backs and shoulders against the wall." (If pressing her back to the wall is too difficult, let her bend her knees.)

2. Say, "Stretch so you are sitting very tall. Keep pushing back so there's hardly any space between your back and the wall. Feel with your hand. Is there any space between your back and the wall?"

3. Say, "Now, let's slide our arms along the wall, up over our heads." Demonstrate.

4. Say, "Now, you do it, too. Great! Now, let's lower our arms very slowly back to the floor."

5. Repeat six times.

Helps Your Child Develop and Enhance …

- Bilateral coordination (for sitting straight in her chair)

- Body awareness (for having her feet on the floor and the cello bow in
  her hand)

- Proprioception (for playing the cello)

Ways to Make It More Challenging

- Have your child inhale as she raises her arms and exhale as she lowers them.

- Have her do the activity in a chair.

What to Look for

- She sits tall with her back close to the wall.

- The upward movement with her arms is smooth and even.

Intermediate

Napkin Origami

What You Need

Napkins

Paper

Pen, pencil, or crayon

What You Do

1. On a piece of paper, draw a rectangle, square, and triangle.

2. Hand your child a napkin. Point to the rectangle and say, "Make the napkin look like this shape."

3. Continue with the square and the triangle.

4. Have him place a folded napkin beside each plate on the table.

Helps Your Child Develop and Enhance ...

- Directionality (for making paper airplanes and origami boats)

- Tactile processing (for discriminating flat surfaces from creased edges)

- Visual processing (for envisioning shapes and letters)

Ways to Make It More Challenging

- Have him direct diners to their seats: "Papa, you get the triangle napkin tonight. Mama, you have the square."

- Suggest more advanced shapes, such as a trapezoid and cylinder.

- Have him fold the napkins without the aid of your pictures.

What to Look for

- Your child folds the napkins according to the shapes you've drawn.

- His folds are smooth.

Intermediate

Paper Balls

What You Need

Scrap paper, 8½ x 11

What You Do

1. Say, "Watch me fold this paper in half." Fold the paper and crease the fold neatly.

2. Say, "Now you take a paper. Fold it and crease it." Make sure she presses the crease firmly.

3. Say, "Watch how I hold my paper with one hand and use the other hand to tear the paper in half. Now I'll fold and crease this piece, and then you do the same with your paper."

4. Have her fold, crease, and tear her paper into smaller and smaller pieces.

5. When your paper is about 2 inches square, say, "I'm going to use just one hand to crumple this piece of paper into a little, tiny ball. Now I'm going to open the paper up, using the same hand. I'm going to crumple it again and squeeze it really tight. Can you do it, too?"

6. Repeat steps #1 through #5 with the other pieces of paper.

7. End with little balls of paper. Throw them at each other.

Helps Your Child Develop and Enhance …

- Laterality (for turning on the faucet)

- Proprioception (for brushing her teeth)

- Tactile processing (for squeezing toothpaste onto her toothbrush)

Ways to Make It More Challenging

- Crumple and uncrumple two pieces of paper, using both hands at the same time.

- Race each other to see who can crumple or uncrumple fastest.

- Use various textures and sizes of paper. Try newspaper, tissue paper, and construction paper.

What to Look for

- She folds the paper accurately.

- She uses both hands appropriately to tear the paper neatly.

- She uses only one hand to manipulate the paper without holding it against her body or any other surface.

          Intermediate

People Obstacle Course

What You Need

Five or six family members and friends

What You Do

1. Say, "Put my body into a position where you can go over me. That's right. Now, go over me."

2. Say, "Now, position me so you can go under me."

3. Continue having your child position other people into obstacles, using various prepositions such as:

- Under
- Around
- Between
- Into and out of

4. Say, "Now, let's put all the people obstacles together. Remember that I'm 'Over,' Grandma is 'Around,'" and so on.

5. Have your child go through the obstacle course he built.

Helps Your Child Develop and Enhance …

- Directionality (for handwriting and math)

- Motor planning (for getting things into and out of a backpack)

- Proprioception (for pushing and holding open a heavy door)

- Spatial awareness (for judging distances on paper)

Ways to Make It More Challenging

Ask your child to go through the obstacle course:

- Backward

- Sideways

- Quietly

- Loudly

What to Look for

- He understands prepositional concepts.

- He demonstrates his intention when positioning people.

Intermediate

Shape Stretch

What You Need

A length of waistband elastic twice the height of the child, securely fastened into a continuous loop

What You Do

1. Give the elastic loop to your child and say, "How many sides does a triangle have? Good. How can you use three body parts to make a triangle?"

2. Repeat, asking your child to use his body to form the loop into a:

- Square
- Rectangle
- Vertical line
- Horizontal line
- Pentagon

Helps Your Child Develop and Enhance …

- Motor planning (for using a compass in geometry class)

- Proprioception (for keeping the compass point in place)

- Visual processing (for reading the protractor angles)

Ways to Make It More Challenging

- Ask your child to draw a shape and then make it with his elastic loop.

- Have him make shapes while lying down.

What to Look for

- He keeps control of the elastic loop.

- He makes the shapes correctly.

Intermediate

Snaky

What You Need

A length of rope about 18 inches long

What You Do

1. Hand the rope to your child and say, "Let's pretend this rope is a friendly snake. Say 'Hello' to your snake."

2. Say, "Put your snake on your shoulder and pet him gently. Now put your snake on your other shoulder."

3. Ask her to show you how she balances her snake on her:

   - Knee
   - Wrist
   - Head
   - Foot

4. Ask her to put her snake on the ground in a straight line and show you how she can:

   - Jump over her snake
   - Jump backward over her snake
   - Walk on her snake

5. Ask her to show you how she makes her snake into these shapes:

   - Circle
   - Triangle
   - Letters of the alphabet

Helps Your Child Develop and Enhance …

- Body awareness (for putting her feet into her sneakers)

- Tactile processing (for adjusting her socks and the tongues of her sneakers)

- Visual processing (for watching how her hands tie the laces, until she has mastered the skill and can do it without looking)

Ways to Make It More Challenging

- Give her two "snakes" and have her repeat all the activities.

- Ask her to crumple her snake in her hand as tightly as she can. Then ask her to drop her snake on the floor. Say, "Can you make your body look like your snake?"

What to Look for

- She follows your directions.

- She easily positions her body and manipulates the rope.

Intermediate

Sound Stretch

What You Need

No equipment

What You Do

1. Say, "Let's say the vowels: A, E, I, O, U. Good, you got it! Now we're going to play with those letters."

2. Ask, "How long can you make the letter 'A' sound last?" Encourage him to sustain the "A" sound for at least 5 seconds.

3. Say, "Now, let's use that same long 'A' sound as we slowly bend over and touch our toes. Great!"

4. Continue matching movement to the sounds, making sure that
   he sustains the vowel sound as he moves:

   - E = knees

   - I = belly button

   - O = chin

   - U = top of the head

Helps Your Child Develop and Enhance ...

- Auditory processing (for learning a new language)

- Body awareness (for putting on costumes)

- Vestibular processing (for flying on an airplane)

Ways to Make It More Challenging

- Have him start the sounds with a consonant,
  such as:

  - S = Say, See, Sigh, Sew, Sue

  - F = Fay, Fee, Fie, Foe, Foo

  - T = Tay, Tee, Tie, Tow, Too

- Correspond different body parts with the sounds.

What to Look for

- His movements and verbalizations are "in sync."

- He sustains the sounds.

Intermediate

Stop It!

What You Need

A tennis ball

What You Do

1. Ask your child to sit on the floor at least 6 feet away from you.

2. Roll the ball from one hand to the other, stopping it by placing your open hand on top of it. Say, "Watch how I stop this ball with my hand."

3. Slowly roll the ball to her and have her stop it by placing her open hand on top of it.

4. Say, "This time, show me how you can stop the ball with your elbow."

5. Repeat the activity, asking her to stop the ball with other body parts, such as chin, knee, and foot.

Helps Your Child Develop and Enhance …

- Body awareness (for knowing which article of clothing goes on which body part)

- Motor planning (for putting the article of clothing on the correct body part)

- Visual processing (for planning her outfit)

Ways to Make It More Challenging

- Roll the ball at different rates of speed.

- Roll the ball slightly to her side, rather than directly to her.

- Have her play the game from a standing position.

What to Look for

- She uses the body part requested.

- She stops the ball accurately.

Intermediate

Stop It, Cup!

What You Need

A tennis ball

Two plastic cups, preferably two different colors

What You Do

1. Ask your child to sit on the floor at least 6 feet away from you.

2. Roll the ball from one hand to the other, stopping it by placing the cup on top of it. Say, "Watch how I stop this ball with the cup."

3. Slowly roll the ball to your child and have her stop it by placing the cup on top of it.

4. Say, "Now hold the cup with both hands. Catch the ball with the cup again." Roll the ball to your child and watch her capture it with both hands on the cup.

5. Give her the other cup and say, "Hold the red cup in one hand and the blue in the other. Now I'm going to tell you which cup to use to catch the ball." Roll the ball and call out, "Blue." Next, roll the ball and call out "Red." Call out the colors in random order.

Helps Your Child Develop and Enhance ...

- Laterality (for taking a tennis ball out of the can)

- Midline crossing (for using a tennis racket)

- Visual processing (for hitting the tennis ball)

Ways to Make It More Challenging

- Roll the ball to the right of her. Ask her to trap it with her opposite hand.

- Vary the speed at which you roll the ball.

- Use "right" and "left" rather than "red" and "blue."

- Add a yellow and a green cup to the red and blue. Have her hold her hands on her head. Call out a color as you roll the ball to her.

What to Look for

- She stops the ball with the cup.

- She uses the correct hand to stop the ball, crossing the midline when appropriate.

- She uses the correct color of cup.

Intermediate

Where Am I?

What You Need

A large box, big enough to hide your child

What You Do

1. Say, "Can you hide inside this box? Make sure all of you is hidden."

2. Say, "Can you put two hands outside the box? Nothing else, just your two hands."

3. Ask your child to put only the following body parts outside the box:

   - Head
   - Elbows
   - Knees
   - Feet and head (nothing else!)

Helps Your Child Develop and Enhance ...

- Body awareness (for playing "Simon Says")

- Motor planning (for playing dodgeball)

- Spatial awareness (for playing hide-and-seek)

Ways to Make It More Challenging

- Use more complex parts or combinations of body parts, such as:

  - One foot and one hand

  - Both elbows and one foot

  - Tummy

  - Tongue

- Reverse the directions and have your child put his body part(s) into the box while he is outside the box.

What to Look for

- He knows the body part(s) requested.

- He maneuvers his body to show just the part(s) requested while keeping everything else hidden.

Intermediate

Zop and Hop

What You Need

No equipment

What You Do

1. Say, "I'll say a nonsense word, 'Zop.' Zop rhymes with another word that means a way of moving. Can you say the word and do the movement? Hop! Right!"

2. Have your child rhyme and demonstrate the movement word, using nonsense words such as:

- Brump - Jump
- Garch - March
- Mun - Run
- Pither - Slither
- Bipboe - Tiptoe

Helps Your Child Develop and Enhance ...

- Auditory processing (for reciting rhymes and telling stories)

- Motor planning (for acting out the characters)

- Proprioception (for putting on costumes)

Ways to Make It More Challenging

- Use nonsense phrases, such as, "Brump on both breet," or "Garch gackward."

- Have your child think up the nonsense words for your responses..

What to Look for

- He recognizes the movement words from your rhyming nonsense words.

- His movements are accurate.

Intermediate

Crossroads

What You Need

Very long rope

What You Do

1. Ask your child to help you stretch the rope out on the floor.

2. Ask her to walk on it from one end to the other. She may be able to balance on it like a tightrope, or she may keep one foot on the rope and the other foot on the floor.

3. Then ask her to make the rope cross at some point.

4. Ask her to walk on it again, from beginning to end. Be sure that she continues on the rope as it crosses over itself, rather than turning at the intersection.

5. Say, "Now can you make the rope cross in two (three, four) places?"

6. Ask her to walk on the rope again, from beginning to end. Be sure that she continues on the rope as it crosses over itself, rather than turning at the intersection.

Helps Your Child Develop and Enhance …

*   Balance (for biking around curves)

*   Midline crossing (for turning the steering wheel to make a U-turn)

*   Spatial awareness (for riding one's bike around traffic cones)

Ways to Make It More Challenging

*   Ask her to jump the course with the rope between her feet.

*   Lay the rope on the floor with many crossings and zigzags.

*   Have her copy the rope path onto a chalkboard or piece of paper.

What to Look for

*   She accurately follows the path at each intersection.

*   She accurately copies the path on paper, noting each intersection, without lifting her pencil.

Jump 'n Spell

What You Need

Chalk

What You Do

1. Draw a "four square" on the ground. Decide with your child which four letters you will use. In this example, we'll use "e," "t," "a," and "m."

2. Say, "Stand on the letter 'm.' Now jump on the letters with both feet to spell the word 'mat.'"

3. Ask her to jump to spell the following words:

• Me	• Eat	• Mate
• Met	• Ate	• Meat
• Mat	• Tea	• Tame

4. Change the letters and have your child jump out new words.

Helps Your Child Develop and Enhance…

- Bilateral coordination (for focusing and holding binoculars)
- Motor planning (for hiking through the forest)
- Visual processing (for spotting and identifying birds)

Ways to Make It More Challenging

- Ask her to hop on one foot.
- Add more squares and letters to make longer words.

What to Look for

- As your child jumps, her feet land at the same time.
- She spells the words correctly.

Plate on Shoe, Do, Do

What You Need

Paper plate

What You Do

1. Give your child a paper plate, and say, "Listen, I'll clap slowly. On the first two claps, I'll tell you something to do. On the second two claps, I'll say, do, do, while you do what I said." Clap steadily and say: "Plate on shoe, do, do."

2. After she practices placing the plate on her shoe, continue clapping and giving simple directions, such as:

   - Plate on   head,   do,   do.
   - Plate on   elbow,   do,   do.
   - Plate under   chin,   do,   do.
   - Plate to   other hand,   do,   do.

3. Let her take a turn to clap and tell you what to do with the paper plate.

Helps Your Child Develop and Enhance …

- Auditory processing (for singing "Frosty the Snowman")

- Body awareness (for dressing a snowman)

- Motor planning (for making a snowman)

Ways to Make It More Challenging

- Speed up the claps and instructions.

- Have her follow instructions while standing on one foot.

- Have her clap and give directions to you.

What to Look for

- She responds promptly and accurately when moving the plate.

- She speaks and claps rhythmically when giving directions.

Advanced

Rise and Shine

What You Need

No equipment

What You Do

1. Say, "Have a seat on the floor. Now, let's think of all the different ways to stand up. Show me how you stand up."

2. After your child scrambles to his feet, ask him to rise in these ways:

   - With just one hand

   - With no hands

   - With his eyes closed

   - While rocking back and forth to get momentum

Helps Your Child Develop and Enhance …

- Motor planning (for learning yoga poses and karate positions)

- Proprioception (for developing endurance and "oomph")

- Vestibular processing (for moving without getting dizzy)

Ways to Make It More Challenging

- Have your child rise from a lying-down position.

- Sit on the floor and press your back against his. Now push against each other to rise.

What to Look for

- He understands the directions.

- He rises in the manner requested.

Advanced

Rocking Boat

What You Need

No equipment

What You Do

1. Ask your child to lie on her stomach and grab her ankles behind her.

2. Say, "Lift your chin and curve your back so just your tummy touches the floor."

3. Ask, "Can you rock back and forth, like a boat?"

Helps Your Child Develop and Enhance …

- Motor planning (for using a Hula-hoop)

- Proprioception (for propelling a scooter)

- Vestibular processing (for enjoying merry-go-rounds and swings)

Ways to Make It More Challenging

- Have her show you how high she can rock.

- Ask her to rock as you sing or chant, "Row, Row, Row Your Boat." How long can she rock?

What to Look for

- Your child grabs her ankles without needing to see them.

- She initiates and maintains the rocking motion.

Advanced

Semaphore

What You Need

Two paper towel tubes, flashlights, or paper plates per person

What You Do

1. Give your child two paper towel tubes and say, "Let's pretend these are flags. We are going to be sailors on two different ships, and we need to talk. We can use these 'flags' in a system called semaphore."

2. Pick up your two "flags" and say, "When you want to get my attention, hold your flags up with straight arms in a V shape and move them up and down at your sides, like this. This movement is called 'Attention!'" Demonstrate.

3. Say, "When I see you, I can tell you with my flags that I am paying attention. This move is called 'Acknowledge' and looks like this, with both arms sticking straight out to the sides." Demonstrate.

4. Say, "Let's try it. Move your flags to get my attention, and I'll acknowledge you. Good. Now I'll get your attention, and you acknowledge me. Great!"

5. Say, "Now, here's how to use semaphore to say, 'Hi.' Both flags go to the right. For 'H,' the right arm is straight out, and the left arm points to the right foot. For 'I,' the right arm goes up diagonally, and the left arm still points to the right foot." I'll show you, and then you do it." Demonstrate:

Advanced

6. Say, "When a sailor is tired of semaphore, he can say, 'Rest,' by crossing the flags in front of his thighs, like this:"

Helps Your Child Develop and Enhance …

- Directionality (for finding his seat at the football stadium)

- Proprioception (for doing the "wave" at the football game)

- Visual processing (for tracking the plays on the field)

Ways to Make It More Challenging

- Have your child learn the letters and numbers of semaphore and have a real conversation. See *www.inquiry.net/outdoor/skills/b-p/signaling.htm* or *www.braingle.com/brainteasers/codes/semaphore.php* for the positions.

- With your child and other family members, make up your own family code, such as:

  - Rolling hands = "Ready to go"

  - Balancing on one foot, other three limbs outstretched = "Let's call Grandma."

What to Look for

- He imitates your positions.

- He moves his "flags" appropriately.

Advanced

Scissor Limbs

What You Need

Miniature or larger trampoline

What You Do

1. Say, "Stand in the middle of the trampoline. Look at me and jump, opening and closing your legs, like scissors. Do not use your arms. Open your legs, close your legs, open your legs, close your legs."

2. Once your child is able to jump in a regular pattern with his legs, say, "Now show me how to jump using just your arms—no legs. Arms up, arms down, arms up, arms down."

3. Once he is able to jump with his arms open and closed, say, "Now let's see a jumping jack, moving your arms and legs together."

Helps Your Child Develop and Enhance…

- Bilateral coordination (for throwing a wet towel over a laundry line)

- Proprioception (for swimming)

- Vestibular processing (for jumping off the diving board)

Ways to Make It More Challenging

- Ask your child to jump in a pattern, such as, "together, together, apart," or "apart, together, together, apart," using just his legs.

- Ask him to jump in a pattern, such as, "down, down, up" or "up, down, down, up," using just his arms.

- Ask him to jump in a reverse jumping jack pattern. When his legs are open, his arms are at his sides; when his legs are closed, his arms are overhead.

What to Look for

- He jumps in a regular pattern, with his legs and arms used separately and together.

- He jumps in the patterns requested.

- He stays centered on the trampoline.

Advanced

Size Wise

What You Need

A piece of string, 12 to 15 inches long

What You Do

1. Say, "Here's a piece of string. I have one, too. We're going to use our strings to measure things we see in this room."

2. Say, "I'm looking across the room at the switch plate. I'm going to use my string to show how wide I think it is." With both hands, hold your string horizontally in front of you to show how wide you think the switch plate is.

3. Walk to the switch plate while holding your string taut to see if your estimate is accurate.

4. Say, "Now it's your turn. Look at that red book on the shelf. Show me with your string how tall you think that book is."

5. Say, "Now, hold your string taut while you walk to the book and measure it with your string. How close were you?"

Helps Your Child Develop and Enhance ...

- Bilateral coordination (for using a shovel)

- Proprioception (for lifting a shovelful of dirt)

- Visual processing (for estimating the size of the hole)

Ways to Make It More Challenging

- Have your child jump to the measured object.

- Ask her to hold her measuring string taut over her head as she moves toward the measured object.

What to Look for

- She is accurate in her measurements.

- She holds the string taut as she moves.

Advanced

Slippy Slidey

What You Need

Paper plate

What You Do

1. Ask your child to stand with one foot on a paper plate.

2. Say, "Slide the plate out toward the side, while we count slowly to four. Now slide it in while we count to four."

3. Next, have her slide the plate in front of her and back to center, and then behind her and back to center, all the while counting slowly.

4. Have her switch feet.

Helps Your Child Develop and Enhance …

- Balance (for staying upright on ice skates)

- Directionality (for making a figure eight)

- Laterality (for skating)

Ways to Make It More Challenging

- Have her slide the paper plate diagonally toward the opposite side of her body, in front and in back.

- Have her squat and stretch her leg longer to slide the plate farther.

- Have her "draw" a circle, triangle, and square with her plate.

What to Look for

- She keeps her balance.

- She slides her foot in and out smoothly.

- She slides the plate as easily with one foot as with the other.

Advanced

Turnstile

What You Need

Miniature or larger trampoline

What You Do

1. Place the mini-trampoline in the center of the room. Choose words for the four directions your child will face as he jumps on the trampoline, such as, "me," "wall," "door," and "table." These will be his "spots."

2. Say, "Stand in the middle of the trampoline. Face me and jump."

3. Say, "Face the wall and keep jumping. Now, keep jumping and turn back to me. Great!"

4. Say, "I'm going to call out the words we talked about. Keep jumping and turn to face each spot as soon as you hear it. Ready? Me, wall. Good! Try this one: Door, wall, me." Allow for a few jumps between each of the "spots." Begin with two-spot directions and add more as your child is ready.

Helps Your Child Develop and Enhance …

- Auditory processing (for passing the salt, instead of the pepper, when asked)

- Bilateral coordination (for carrying a platter to the table)

- Directionality (for knowing which way to pass the platter)

- Vestibular processing (for sitting comfortably at the table)

Ways to Make It More Challenging

- Use longer sets of directions.

- Use right and left instead of descriptive words.

What to Look for

- Your child is accurate in the direction he moves.

- He jumps on both feet simultaneously.

Advanced

Wall Ball

What You Need

Masking tape

Tennis ball

A wall that masking tape won't damage

What You Do

1. On the wall, place a straight, horizontal line of masking tape, at least 6 feet long, at your child's shoulder height.

2. Hand her a tennis ball. Point to the starting end of the tape on the left and say, "Show me how you can roll this ball along the tape all the way to the end, using your hands."

3. Once she has successfully traced the tape with her ball several times, have her pull off the tape and make a sticky wad. Save the sticky wads for a fun surprise at the end.

4. Continue placing the tape on the wall in different ways:

- Curvy line

- Vertical line (beginning within arm's reach, all the way to the floor)

- Two vertical, parallel lines—have her use both hands to move two balls from top to bottom.

5. Have her collect all the sticky wads. Say, "Show me how you can squish all this tape into one big ball. Now let's play 'catch!'"

Helps Your Child Develop and Enhance …

- Directionality (for writing in cursive)

- Proprioception (for squeezing paint out of the tube)

- Tactile processing (for handling classroom tools, such as scissors and crayons)

- Visual processing (for writing on lined paper)

Ways to Make It More Challenging

- Ask your child to move the ball along the line by using one hand at a time. Be sure she repeats it with the other hand.

- Make the masking tape line angular rather than curvy.

- Have her place the tape on the wall in her own way.

What to Look for

- She keeps the ball on the line.

- She is aware of the changes in the line.

Advanced

About the Authors

Joye Newman is a perceptual motor therapist. Perceptual motor therapy (PMT) helps children and adults develop and enhance basic movement and learning abilities. In 1979, Joye earned her master's degree in education and human development from George Washington University, with a specialty in perceptual motor development. Joye integrated studies in behavioral optometry, occupational therapy, and psychology into her graduate work and developed her own unique method of PMT.

Joye founded and continues to direct a popular organization called Kids Moving Company (KMC). She began KMC because she was concerned that many kids were not encouraged to move around at home and school—in fact, she found that many kids were discouraged from moving. She wanted to provide a place for children to move, play, and think in a developmentally appropriate environment. Originally, KMC offered fun and functional activities, PMT, and birthday parties for children in a studio setting. Today, the studio portion of KMC has been closed as Joye focuses on in-school programs, individual evaluations, and consultations with parents to help them understand how they can help their children become more confident and competent in everything they do.

Joye was a founding member and the original education chair of Washington Independent Services for Educational Resources (WISER), a cofounder of the Jewish Primary Day School of Washington, DC, and an early childhood special-needs consultant for the Board of Jewish Education. She lectures on school readiness, creative movement, and perceptual motor development in her consultations with area preschools to help them develop and refine their movement programs. Joye lives in Maryland and has three grown children. Her Web site is www.kidsmovingco.com.

Carol Kranowitz was a music and movement teacher at St. Columbia's Nursery School in Washington, DC, for 25 years. During that time, she observed many "out-of-sync" preschoolers who seemed uncomfortable or clumsy and had trouble with ordinary activities, such as walking across the playground, holding hands, playing circle games, and going through obstacle courses. To help these children become more competent at work and play, Carol began to study a relatively common disability called Sensory Processing Disorder (SPD). SPD causes difficulties in the interpretation and use of sensory messages, such as sensations of touch, balance, and movement, and inhibits a person's ability to function smoothly in daily life.

In the 1980s, Carol began screening preschoolers for SPD with the help of an occupational therapist. They guided children with probable SPD into occupational therapy, which is the primary treatment for this disorder. They steered other children with perceptual motor problems (and possible SPD) into purposeful physical activities, best found at organizations such as Joye Newman's Kids Moving Company.

Carol earned her bachelor's degree at Barnard College and her master's in education and human development at George Washington University. She authored *The Out-of-Sync Child* and *The Out-of-Sync Child Has Fun* and coauthored *Growing an In-Sync Child* with Joye Newman, all published by Perigee. Her other materials, including *The Goodenoughs Get In Sync* and *Preschool SENSE*, are Sensory World publications. In her writings and international workshops, Carol explains to parents, educators, and other professionals how sensory issues play out. She suggests enjoyable strategies for addressing these issues at home and school. Carol is a board member of The Sensory Therapy And Research (STAR) Center. She lives in Maryland and has five grandchildren. Her Web site is www.out-of-sync-child.com.

The following is a special excerpt
from a related book

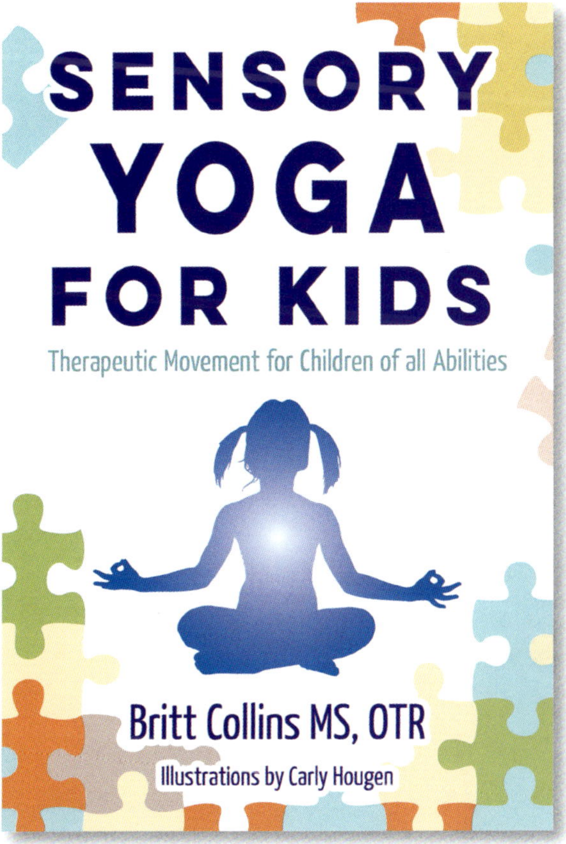

SENSORY YOGA FOR KIDS

Therapeutic Movement for Children of all Abilities

Britt Collins MS, OTR

Illustrations by Carly Hougen

www.SensoryWorld.com

Also available at

A s follows, we will describe each pose and summarize its benefits. Later these poses will be put into various suggested sequences to help meet the specific needs of your child. This chapter intends to define and describe each pose individually so you can have all poses organized in one place. As you read, you will find which areas of challenge most affect your child that particular day or time and can then use that sequence of poses to help your child.

Breathing Techniques

- *Alternate Nostril Breathing*

  Sit comfortably in Easy Pose or kneeling position. Start by placing your left hand on your thigh with the thumb and index finger touching. Then take your right hand up to your face. Your right thumb is gently touching your right nostril and your right ring finger is gently touching the left nostril. You are not using your index and middle finger; they can gently rest in between your eyebrows or tuck them in. Close your right nostril with your thumb and inhale through your left nostril for 4 counts and then close left nostril and open right nostril. Exhale out of the right nostril for 4 counts, inhale through the right nostril and then exhale through the left nostril. Try this up to 8 rounds if you can. If a child restricts their breath then stop. This should be easy for the child.

*This is said to be one of the most calming exercises for the nervous system.

- *Bumblebee Breath*

  Hold a flower in your hand or a pretend flower, breath in through your nose and then hum as you breath out making a buzzing bee noise. Try making higher-pitched buzzing, then lower-pitched buzzing.

- *Bellows Breath*

  When starting Bellows Breath, start by sitting with your spine straight in an effortless posture. You can do this while sitting cross-legged on the floor with a blanket underneath your sitting bones, or you can sit in a chair with your back straight. Both the inhalation and exhalation are forceful and have equal emphasis (you can hear it out your nose as your stomach presses in and out). Sometimes it is nice to start by placing your hands on your stomach to feel your breath going in and out. Each inhalation and exhalation is at the rate of 1 per second, so you start out slowly with 10 breaths. Then take a few resting breaths and then try 10 more breaths. You can speed up your bellows breath and then slow it down again at the end. Make sure the child does not report or look lightheaded when breathing quickly this way until she is used to practicing this.

- *Volcano Breath*

  Stand in Mountain Pose, bring hands to heart center, inhale reach arms up, then as you exhale bend forward and exhale all your breath making an Ahhh sound like an erupting volcano. Repeat 2-3 times.

- *Mindful Breathing*

  Mindfulness is discussed more in Chapter 12, but I want to describe it here as well, because it will show up in some of the yoga sequences as a beginning activity for increasing awareness, grounding, calming and regulating the nervous system. Mindful breathing is being aware of your current breath, feeling how you normally breathe and paying attention to how your breath feels. Is it warm or cool; do you feel it coming in through the nostrils, down the throat and into your lungs? Do not change your breath; just be aware of how you are breathing, while either sitting in a chair or on the floor in a mindful body position.[7]

Eye Exercises

There are many benefits that yoga provides for our eyes, and you can do eye exercises to help strengthen and rejuvenate them. One is to sit in Easy Pose, relax your body and take several deep breaths. Then rub your hands together several times, creating heat in your hands, and then place the palms of your hands over your eyes so that all you see is dark. Relax and allow the heat from your palms to relax your eyes. Hold this position for 10-15 seconds.

Another great eye exercise is to look straight ahead and then pretend there is a clock in front of you. Think of looking at 12, 3, 6, 9 and back to 12 (without moving your head) and then to 3, 6, 9 and back to 12. Then repeat in the opposite direction. If you are working with a young child, you can sit in front of him with a pencil that has a cute eraser on the end of it and have him hold his head still and follow your pencil through the clock positions. This helps strengthen the eye muscles. After doing this exercise, practice the palm-to-eyes position again to relax them and keep them shut for 10-15 seconds.

Alphabetical list of yoga poses

When practicing with children, we want to make sure they are in good alignment, but we know they are wiggly little creatures, and this can sometimes be hard. Try to model good posture positions for them, and if they are young or have a physical disability, you will help them move into and out of the poses safely. The descriptions will help you know how to assume the pose and then assist those who need it. If possible, its best to allow the child to imitate you unless you are worried she will hurt herself, then please physically help cue her into the correct position. If you are unsure of any poses and the safety of them with your child, skip that pose and ask a professional yoga instructor how to help guide you.

1. Bridge Pose

Lie on your back, bend your knees, and place your feet flat on the floor. Bring your heels closer to your buttocks and extend your arms  down by your side. Then, when you are ready, lift your hips off the ground slowly while breathing.

If you are assisting a child in this pose, sit to the side of him and help hold his feet on the ground while slowly lifting underneath his lower back/hips. If his feet lifts or slides, then lower his hand on his back so you are not pulling him up too high. Be careful you are not hurting his neck or that, if he is doing this alone, his head and neck are aligned with the body.

Benefits:
- Improves circulation
- Improves digestion
- Stretches neck, chest, hips and spine
- Strengthens hamstrings and buttocks
- Reduces headaches

2. Bow Pose

Lie on your tummy, arms down by your side, palms facing up. Take 2-3 slow deep breaths. As you exhale, bend your knees, bringing your heels as close to your bottom as you can. Reach back and grab your ankles. If this is as far as you can go, that is fine; if you can go further, inhale and lift your heels away from your bottom, pulling your chest and head up. Make sure your shoulders are relaxed. Be sure to keep breathing.

Alternative poses: Half bow – You can help a child by helping her reach her arms back to hold her ankles, or you can bend her knees and gently hold them for her while she is lying on her tummy. Be careful not to overstretch the quadriceps muscles if they are tight.

You can also just bend one leg at a time while the child is lying on her tummy and stretch their quadriceps until she is ready to go to the next step.

Do not do this yourself or with a child if you have lower back pain.

Benefits:
- Improves circulation
- Improves digestion
- Strengthens the back and increases flexibility in the back
- Stretches the entire front of the body, including neck and chest
- Improves function of liver, pancreas and large and small intestines

3. Butterfly (bound angle pose)

Start by sitting on your buttocks with both legs straight out in front of you. Then bring both legs in, with the soles of the feet touching. You can have a folded blanket underneath your buttocks if needed for comfort. Bring your heels as close to your pelvis as you can, and relax your knees as they fall to the sides. They do not have to touch the floor. If this is an uncomfortable pose to hold for long, you can place folded blankets under each knee to make this more relaxing. Make sure your back is straight.

Be cautious if you have a knee injury.

Benefits:
- Improves circulation
- Helps with anxiety and fatigue
- Stimulates abdominal organs
- Stretches groin and thighs

4. Cat/Cow Pose

Begin on your hands and knees with a neutral back (table pose), then take a breath in, sink your tummy down towards the floor, bring your head up and look forward. Then as you exhale, round your back, tuck your tailbone, and look down towards the floor. Continue cat/cow stretches following your breathing for 5-7 breaths.

Benefits:
- Strengthens and stretches the spine
- Stretches tummy, hips and back
- Creates emotional balance
- Massages the internal organs

5. Chair Pose

Start in Mountain Pose, inhale, reach the arms up, and either connect the hands or face the palms in. As you exhale, bend your knees like you are sitting in a chair and try to get your thighs parallel to the floor. Your knees will slightly reach over your toes. Activate your thigh muscles and squeeze your shoulder blades slightly.

Take caution with this pose if you have low blood pressure or a headache

Benefits:
- Strengthens thighs, calves, ankles and back

- Helps build core strength
- Helps work on balance
- Stretches shoulders and chest
- Stimulates abdominal organs and heart

6. Child's Pose

Kneel and sit back on your heels, then slightly open your knees so your big toes are touching behind you. Lean forward so your forehead is touching the ground and reach your arms out in front of you. You can also relax your arms by your side. This is a resting pose.

Benefits:
- Stretches the spine
- Releases tension in the back
- Calms the mind (which reduces stress) and encourages strong breathing
- Improves circulation, which reduces headaches

7. Cobra Pose

Lie on your stomach on the floor with your legs stretched out with the tops of the feet on the floor. Bring your hands up by your shoulders, keep your elbows close to your body, and then inhale and gently press your torso up only as far as your lower back will allow. You can press up to where you have a soft bend in the elbows. Keep your pelvic bones on the floor and try to relax your buttocks. Hold for 10-15 seconds and exhale, coming back to the floor.

> *Do not do this pose if you have a back injury, carpal tunnel syndrome or a headache*
> *Alternatives for this could be Sphinx Pose—see below.*

Benefits:
- Stimulates abdominal muscles

- Opens heart and lungs
- Lengthens the spine and strengthens the back
- Therapeutic for asthma
- Stretches chest, shoulders and back
- Strengthens arms
- Increases flexibility
- Improves digestion
- Elevates mood

8. Crescent Moon Pose

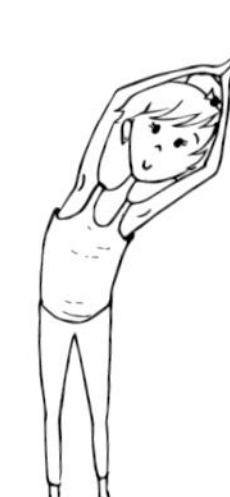

Start in Mountain Pose, inhale and reach overhead. Interlock your fingers, keeping your index fingers pointed toward the sky. Exhale and stretch over to the right, pressing your hip opposite towards the left. Hold this for 10-15 seconds, then straighten the back to standing, and bring hands to heart center. Repeat on the other side.

If you are helping a child do this, make sure you gently guide him through the arch and prevent him from bending forward. Do not push him past his comfort zone.

You may also do this pose seated for those children who have physical disabilities or those children who struggle with standing balance.

Benefits:
- Improves balance and core strength
- Increases circulation
- Improves flexibility of spine
- Promotes kidney function

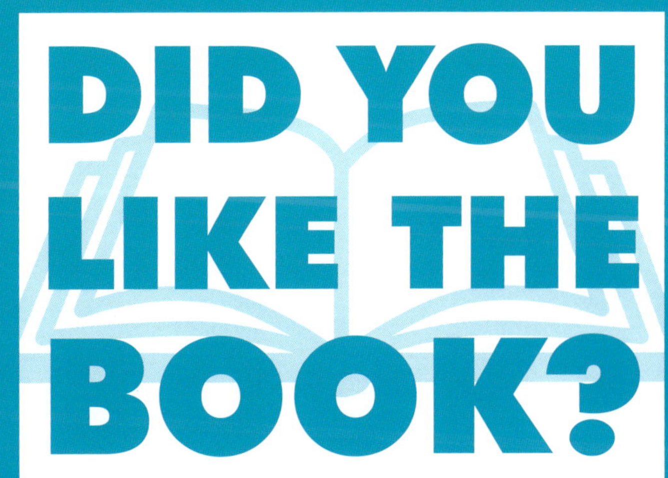

Not what you expected? Tell us!

Most negative reviews occur when the book did not reach expectation. Did the description build any expectations that were not met? Let us know how we can do better.

Please drop us a line at *info@fhautism.com*.

Thank you so much for your support!